SHINDIG

D1428386

GLYN WRIGHT

Shindig

BLOODAXE BOOKS

ISBN: 1 85224 409 7

First published 1997 by
Bloodaxe Books Ltd,
P.O. Box 1SN,
Newcastle upon Tyne NE99 1SN.

Bloodaxe Books Ltd acknowledges
the financial assistance of Northern Arts.

Cover printing by J. Thomson Colour Printers Ltd, Glasgow.

Printed in Great Britain by
Cromwell Press Ltd, Broughton Gifford, Melksham, Wiltshire.

Acknowledgements

'The Blacksmith's New Song' was originally published in *Smith's Knoll*, 'The Nature Boys' in *Smoke*, and 'Fantasies' in *Iron*. 'Shindig' was a prizewinner in the 1994 Charterhouse International Poetry Competition.

Contents

Cod

The birds of dusk have abandoned chimney pots.
Cats haunt shadows of the alleys, and knuckly accents
Tear up language where the street gives way to dark.
In the room of claret and grape: overtures of anticipation;
Orchestral voices beckon you to regions of luxuriance,
Sing: Come follow the flute player, journey out,
Walk in the garden of poppy and rose, stroll
With fiddlers in the lush grass, whose moonlit paths
Will bring you out to yet more gorgeous zones
Of wild sweet honey where skin becomes fur.

As hurrying feet claim back the street's damp slabs
And printed flowers make muted blossom,
And sky is grey tile walked upon by muddy paws,
You are mongrel, alleycat: skin of old rung, binbag mouths.
Your rattled exchanges echo crockery and spoon
While bowed strings speak of creatures
That will yearn, brew tea, share a newspaper
Whose cartoonist offers penguins that ape magnates
And dream of penthouses with swimming pools
Shaped like plaice and cod.

Shindig

When scallywags throw a jagged arc across the road
it seems we're in a movie no one made. For here
is where cameras seek out pictures that will say:
Look, look, this is where all things break up.

Light-footed in our party shoes we shuffle free
from bad-eyed boys, skip away down binbag alleys
that angle us by turns to number five, where
the massed generations of McCalls are having a do.

Two aunts out front, slow river as grey backdrop,
sip wine, pinching long-stemmed glasses, lament
in whispers a street of unscrubbed doorsteps,
a crop of kids who don't know how to play.

Before coarse, booming speakers, the painted girls,
dancing without their mouthy, lumpish lads,
circle bare creaking boards, clapping out lost words
beneath blue and purple flashing lights.

A scrum of hairdos by the food inhale heady scandal,
share out the big cream buns of tasty news.
And someone says, 'She's done so well. Let's hope
she'll not forget just where it was she started from.'

As whippersnappers hide and seek in leggy forests,
a creased face talking smoke recalls a game called locusts,
an organ-grinder with a rude red monkey,
a parrot Billy Mac brought home from sea.

Fast-flowing ale and spirits erode silences
and stony grudges, sweep through part-silted veins.
And there beneath the paper roses, the tinsel moons,
a powdered crone wails *My Way* in a quavering out-of-tune.

Old uncles: former sailors, boilermakers, skivvies,
their bellies belted, lean together out in the yard,
raise fat-fingered cans, fisted tankards,
cheer and whoop the flashbulb like a stripper.

Around the big glass and tincan mountain, big lads,
easy now in stout arms and legs, kiss upturned bottles
with zip and swagger. And a low voice by the stairs
intones, 'She has done well. What a pity she's not here.'

'I knew a woman in Libraville,' confesses wistful Billy Mac,
shrunk now inside his shiny-legged best suit.
But here the dance goes on, here the aches are sweated off
as the floorboards bounce to roaring shindig sounds.

Hot bodies in their holiday shirts and rag-silk dresses
are wrapped around by smoke and scent, chatter and guitars,
but the old brass clock's kept up a muted backbeat on the wall,
and now its short sharp hands begin that late unravelling.

And someone says, 'She's done so well,' as hammer rhythms
drum us to the door where we arrange our own costumes,
prepare for streets where we'll resume our roles
as bit-part players in the night-scenes of a creaking city.

Breaking

The pavement is crazy with fractures,
The shelter surrounded by petrified tears.
Cats withdraw down alleyways. A Rover
Eases predatory from a side road.

A crane ticks, chained ball a pendulum
Crashing through the clockcase.
As bricks explode a dustcloud forms
And rubble's dry rain begins to fall.

There are men in the road digging graves:
Earthquake and machine-gun fire. Kids
Are grubs in gutters; blasting the ghetto
They spin to make the world revolve.

But here is a surgeon tending a bike,
Outfit laid on weedy gravel:
Adhesive, patches, connection,
Thumbs massaging the tyre's pink flesh.

Time

They built a new pub with no piano, thumping din.
I watched the steel ball swinging from a cable.
The crane would tick out there for hours and then
a sudden crash as walls exploded into rubble.

After grumbling choruses of mean machines,
shrieking operas of drills that gave no peace,
six days of clock and hooter and grumpy boss,
you had soft tinkled notes in the Half Way House,
pianist doing requests of you hummed the tunes.

Years drift like dust, then voices call from wayback.
Odd days a scrap of song won't leave me be. I hear
pale girls, see the shape of words on mouths of lipstick;
fellahs scrubbed of muck, white shirts and glossy hair,
swaying along the polished benches, just the same
every Saturday night until yer man called time.

Shanghai Jack

Shanghai Jack would dance a hornpipe
In the road outside the dock.
When his puppet danced before him
He sang tales of Captain Hook.

Jack pulled strings and took you with him
Round the world and back again:
Spicy Islands, pigtail pirates,
Places stranger then the moon.

Mother took me every Friday
To stand outside the big dock gate.
We would wait with other women
Till the crowd of men rushed out.

When my dad came she would stop him,
Block his pathway to The Goat;
She would stay there till he'd handed
Money so that we could eat.

I would say: Oh, please don't take me
'Cause I feel such awful shame,
Children mock me in the playground
'Cause my dad drinks all the time.

You must come with me, she'd say,
You must do it for my sake,
And then you'll get your favourite treat:
We'll go one day to Shanghai Jack.

So, down I went and did my duty,
Then up in bed long into night
I'd be woken by a racket:
Dad come singing down the street.

He was life-breath of all parties
When he was topped up with ale;
Put a pint pot in his big fist
And he became the sparky fool.

When a seaman took his pay-off
After months on board a ship,
Our front room was ideal venue
For his welcome home booze-up.

Stale tobacco in the morning,
Beery bottles on the floor,
Turned my stomach, made me vow to
Move a hundred miles from there.

I would say: I'll go forever,
No I'm never coming back;
I will find a leafy village
Many miles from any dock.

But the sound of distant voices
Floats from far to these low hills.
I hear some days the big ships' fog horns,
Milligan's banjo, seabird calls.

I catch old Jack's voice singing to me:
Down the years his tunes come drifting:
Songs of strange lands and the ocean;
Newfoundland and old Hong Kong.

No, I say, now that's all over.
No, I say, now leave me be Jack,
'Cause I'm never, never ever,
No, I'm never coming back.

In the Time of Noise

Drill and dogbark. The shutter clatter.
Clapped-out engine groaning by.
Screechbrake. Hammer. Stereodrumbeat.
Throbbing 'copter in the sky.

What I was trying to say was that.
What I was trying to say. BANG!
D-I-Y is. D-I-Y is. D-I-Y is doing in
your head. Headache. Lawnmower. Clang!

Toot toot. Beep beep. GET OUTA MY WAY!
What. What I was trying to.
Drillbit chewing up the masonry
as if the dentist is after you.

The paramedic. The fire brigade.
The ice cream van. The car door slam.
The burglar bell, the burglar bell. *What*
I was trying to. Say. What. Bedlam.

The Bass Guitar

Once we had the songs of thrushes, footsteps and teacups.
I made a lily pond. Swarms around the butterfly bush.
You could sit out, breathe honeysuckle and peace.

Next door seems like danceclub-kennel-garage now.
I get his late horror. My own pictures flashing.

Satan plays a bass guitar, whips you with metal strings.
Throbbing in my cushions, beneath plates and floorboards.
It's in the air, in my chest, taunting me for kicks.

If there's a polite way of asking, I've tried it.
But when I phone for help the ringing tone goes on and on.
So I grip the pillow, as a spike is hammered through my head.

In my insomniac dream I saw a whiplash of lightning
strike his amplifier and send a snake of massive volts
biting at his heart. His big frame glowed with the fires
of agony. And I was in some apple garden of delight.

The Rhythm Chamber

Don't let the dawn sneak in here, our rhythm chamber,
with its threats of poison cells or hit-and-run,
satellite voices crying over poisoned lakes.
                                          No.
Don't let it come flying in through doors or glass,
not here where the fast beat echoes in your heart
as you lift away on wings of drumskin,
moving out for gold, wheeling around the moon
until the vast dark blue-black waves of space
carry you, ferry you to galaxies of otherwhere
whose light warm showers will feed you nectar
from the saffron flowers of paradise.
                                      No. No.
Don't let the dawn come near our pulsing bubble,
let it leave us drifting on those boundless tides.
Tell the stone-eyed bouncers to swing their hawk tattoos
when it tries to fly in here.
                                  No. No. No.
No. Please don't let it hunt us down
with that ever-sharpening light.

Children's Party

I dream of Wonderland Park,
a place of bouncy castles
and sky-high helter skelters
where you only have to pay once
and they give special mystery prizes
every night in the Pleasure Dome
and the Karaoke Hall.

You do guitar sounds with your throat,
and French kissers put their tongue in.
They close their eyes all smoochie
and then some go all the way;
which is either gorgeous like heaven
or not as good as shopping.

Round here walls with spiky heads
talk hate and shout bully names
in different colour paint.
Alleyways smell of dog and bones
of yesterday and years ago,
and pavements are covered
in bottlenecks and last week's news,
and footprints you can't see
where all the dead people walked.

We build a den out by the tip
where birds do songs
and moggies play at tigers.

Inside we do snogging
and dreamtalk and movie rap.
We light up and do rings
and keep our lips round
to do blackbird sounds
and wild guitars and choruses
and cats that live out in the dark.

Lesson

the mist was a shaken tambourine
clackers made early morning rain

the drum of the sun came pushing through
till held up high – a silent O

then the flowers of dawn bloomed gong by gong
and triangular birds began to sing

but the bumble bee came rattling down
as if it were a bouncing stone

so the wooden jay went ak-ak-ak
went giggling up and down the blocks

till all three Rs began to RRR-i-i-i-i-ing
as the lesson bell let go its tongue.

Windows are fixed tight shut here. Like walls of wired ice.
But if I press my face hard against the cold, I see
brilliant shapes in strips of purple sky.
And the moon changes from a ball to a silver brooch.

I made brilliance. Turned crazy daydreams into flames.
I said, 'Screw you,' to the dark that creeps out
every night from cupboards behind teacher's desk.
That's where it lives. I know. I've been there.

Bulldog Heath said, 'Can't? There's no such word.'
And I said, 'There is.' And he said, 'Spell it.'
So I said, 'See you en tee.' His hand was a tennis racket
swung for my face till it jerked back just before the hit.

So he shoved me into that little box that has no light.
Just dark. It pokes you in the eye, slides its
fingers around your neck, leans hard against you
to make you not breathe. It nearly makes you piss.

Bongo Greene said, 'Come in and join the group.'
And Lizzie Paintbrush said, 'I like your reds.
And, oh, is your mum any better?' But Bulldog said,
'Bright spark. No, I don't think so.' And slammed the door.

I split a pack of hard bevvy, dragon juice, guzzled it.
Glug-glugged it down my burning throat,
past my belt buckle, right the way down to my socks.
Man, my toes were sizzling, and my heart was a bonfire.

Man, I was big. I was hot, and I was fierce.
Man-oh-man-oh-man, I was the biggest.
I was the hottest. I was the fiercest. I was IT.
And my eyes were flashing up the wildest pictures.

I sucked the juice from Harpo's tank; was only shadow
as I went to work with strikers and a squeezie bottle.
I was less than shadow, not even footprint.
I was the sound of no one passing. In baseball boots.

Creeping like the invisible scallywag I went,
'Ho ho,' to the classroom of chairs, all sitting
to attention before the Bulldog's fatarse throne.
I give each keyhole a squeeze, every gap and cranny.

I spelled SPECIMEN in squirts on the big doors,
then my striker done a curve, and the juice
wuffs like a dog with a cough.
And I give it legs, going, 'Run-run,' in my head.

And then I turn and open my teeth and let out
the gobful of laughs that tickle my tongue,
and say, 'Numbskull. Nitwit. Bright Spark.' And watch
my great red hand crackle up to claw the darkness down.

Eight o'clock, they battered the door. And my head was a drum.
And my eyes were broken glass. And my throat was ashes.
And my ma was saying, 'No, no, not my lad. A mistake.
He wouldn't. He couldn't. And I haven't been well.'

And my head was a tin being hit with a stick.
And then she shouted up like her voice was cracked.
And the glass in my eyes started turning to water.
'Come down,' she called. 'Come down. Come down. Come down.'

THIRD VOICE:

I tasted smoke, saw the burned bones of our block,
heard Ms Greene say *waste* with a hiss and a tut.
She'd start the rhythm going, then you'd join in,
one by one, beating or blowing or just calling out.

In the yard, bigmouths throw filth, nasty names.
But she would say: Look always up and never down.
She won't stand messing, but once she had a lovebite.
And she lends me her own books about the Cosmos.

I'd go in there like a small thing and get strength:
the beat wrapped round you, went through your skin,
and made you go all strange inside your belly.
I was not me any more with spots and pointy nose.

I was part of that big sound we sent out through
high open windows to spread over rooftops
and float away, rising through fields of vapour
and years of light, beyond our stars and moon.

To tell the galaxies: We are here. To tell
the Clouds of Magellan, the Great Spiral in Andromeda,
those glowing distant quasars: We are here
and we are calling; we are weak and we are strong.

Banging On, Banging Off

My old man used a muscle machine,
checked me with the back of his hand.
When I first tuned into rhythm, he said: Off.
He said: Off, off, off; off or I'll clip your ear.
When I beat upon an applebox
he said: Stop. He said: Stop that now.
Said: Stop that, shut that, dreadful row,
and if you don't I'll tan your hide,
I'll thrash, thump, smack, belt,
I'll knock your little headlights out.

When I brought home a bright pink shirt, he said: Nah,
be a man; be a man, be a man, be a man my lad,
be a rock hard man not a nancy boy,
be a mallet and not a custard tart,
put up your fists and lead with your left,
and when you get on top don't stop, don't stop,
don't never never never never stop, till you've won.

When I wore my pink and tapped on tins
he called me cissy, puffdah, fruit.
I used to hear him through the dark
full of ale and hot brown sauce.
When he called me the button on a big girl's blouse
I'd dive inside the sheets and hate;
and though I wept I would not break,
would not, could not, never break,
but whispered *moron* to the pillow:
moron, loudmouth, mallet-head.

I escaped into an attic and lived among my kit:
snare and cymbal, big brass gong,
bongo, bass and kettledrum.
I rolled to somewhere far away, far, far away,
slept between marimba and a dark-skinned tambourine.

Now I see his big hands clapping when I do a gig.
I see him standing back of crowds
and hear him crying: Sorry, I'm sorry lad,
it's a weeping shame when kin fall out.
But I beat on to hammer his voice,
pound on and on so I don't hear his sad old tune,
though I know that I should stop.
Yes, I know that I should stop.
Stop, stop.
       Yes, I know.
             Stop. Stop.
                   Stop.

Trapped

Brian was in love with John, and John was a wild one
like myself. I wore high heel boots and my collar up,
and wouldn't be boxed in. I said to our Julie, 'It was
all about not living trapped like your parents had done.'

I used to dodge off school to hang out down the Cavern
where the walls were sticky from smoke and sweat, and once
I saw real Beats chanting poems outside, but most times
lads from the warehouse would pelt you with rotten fruit.

And once, we all thought Paul was dead, and as far as John
was concerned he might as well have been 'cause he never
forgave him for stealing the spotlight over the break-up;
which was sad, but not half as sad as John getting shot.

And George wasn't wet or sad or haunted like people said.
He gave you raunchy licks and wild boogying kicks,
and the way he comes sliding down them notes on Nowhere Man
is sacred, and on Taxman he gets so riled and hunky.

She seemed to be listening, our Julie, she had this look
on her face as if she was hearing something really good,
which got to me because it's my life and I don't want it
to be lost, and it was a hell of a time to be young.

And they were the greatest band the world has ever known.
And they did give us songs that will live for ever.
She said 'Dad?' I said, 'What, love?' She said, 'So…
does that mean it's okay for me to dodge off school?'

Manners

Our cellar hummed of rats, something gone bad.
Milligan's pawnshop whiffed of mothballs,
and Dada breathed beer fumes on Friday night,
but the smell of Ma's baking was always best.

Dada said women were ladies, and ladies were angels,
but they weren't practical like men, so I must be good,
and talk nicely, and remember my manners, and maybe,
just maybe, I'd get a new white dress
for the May procession of the Virgin Mary.

When he came home singing *The Green Hills of the Highlands*
you knew there'd be two days of peace in the house.
There'd be stories and music and sweet fruity pastry,
and food on the table right through the week.

When he came home singing *Oh Molly It Wasn't My Fault*,
you knew there were tears and long silences brewing.
Ma would touch my hair and say: Go hide down below love,
your effing useless Dada has gone and pissed the housekeeping
up against that stinking alehouse wall again.

Buffer

Father smelled of hair oil and tobacco,
and wound the brass ship's clock on Sundays.
Evenings, he'd talk old times when you wanted
peace, sing music hall songs to his wireless.

One day he spoke of a fire in his chest,
of some beast sucking all his air out.
He would scrape the chair arm with his nails
as he slowly grew too small for his bones.

You'd hear gasps and moans, and then his eyes
stayed closed and his throat began to rattle.
One time I whispered: Go now, please, so that you
will groan no more and I won't have to listen.

When he had gone there seemed more shadow,
cloud and dark. You'd have to use the radio
to smother the rush of your breath, the tick,
tick, tick of the living-room clock.

Crunch

Silence throbs in through gaps under doors.
You are not here to call me fusspot, nuisance,
to walk with me down the creaking steps of years.
Your shrubs scratch now unpruned at the fence.

What was, is you tying new shoots on to canes,
is you talking the life you had before I led you here –
how days were boats that moored in many a harbour.
What was, is your lips shaped to the words of old tunes.

Here will always be the sound of you not pushing your
key in the lock while I sit here waiting. But, no. I won't.
The sea can't be that small. No. I think I hear
my shoes crunching off down the stony path out front.

A Body of Men

It's time for a clampdown. These young bucks need
reigning in, smartening up. And I know exactly how:
conscription. It should never have been scrapped.
That'd knock 'em into shape. *Pick up your kitbag now...*

We cut each other's arms with my grandad's knife,
earned pennies for shifting casks of fish in brine,
and sneaked into shindigs where his uncle played banjo.
Pick up your kitbag now and stand in line...

We'd long been blood brothers when our war came.
He volunteered when I got the call up. South Africa
was first stop: swimming off the Cape of Good Hope.
He had a fine build on him. *La la la-la-la lah...*

But a cracked bone held me back when Jack marched out
to fight the good fight on a battlefield of sand.
He was ambushed some bloody place between
Tripoli and Nowhere. *Turn back for one last time and...*

Living alone has its drawbacks, but I've got memories.
A man was a man in them days. He wasn't girlish or workshy.
You were a body of men, real men, and you were mates.
For one last time and wave your sweetheart goodbye.

Brass Keys

I glimpsed the brass keys glinting in the fire,
Saw ghosts of those who spat on superstition:
Dialectical men who marched out front
Kissing the trombones and tubas of tradition.

I read in coal a tale of struggle: red banner days,
And tunnels of black rock which all refused to enter;
Big Hewer, the flying pickets, and the ace tactician,
The cold-shouldered scab and the Staunch Dissenter.

I saw bandsmen march through history and flames
Towards some vague point where burnt-out systems crash;
Touching notes of keen resistance they went striding on,
Ever onwards, utopia-bound, into smoke and into ash.

The Blacksmith's New Song

We played in barns far from any road, cocking
musical snooks at the one who'd pronounced old songs
not relevant: said we must study his
Collected Thoughts and look to our glittering future

in the damp concrete towers he'd stacked us in.
He took away our children. In barrack-schools
they learnt the silent footwork of gymnastics;
the best were sent to somersault for gold.

We practised old and secret finger tricks,
played wild goat dances, ancient harvest songs
on dulcimer, flute and fiddle.
When the singing cobbler died his son returned,

brought back perfume for his armpits, whispers
of revolt, a hunting rifle that made ours
look like pistols, and a contraption we knew only
from frightening rumours: a piano accordion.

It covered him from chin to balls, outstretched
his arms, squeaked and moaned, honked and farted.
We told him no, the old tunes were not suited
to such a noise-box, made him creak and hee-haw solo.

When the revolt crackled across the north
a chorus filled the square, demands painted on old
bedsheets, and the cobbler's rifle barked, scattering
pigeons for miles, as police threw away their uniforms.

When word came that the president had gone
to learn the music of the sewers, some folk
sat their scented hero on a throne of shoulders,
said he must never again be made to perform alone.

We no longer play in secret, but a pace behind
his heaving back as he flaps cocky elbows
and his box bellows like a knackered bull,
brays like a donkey with the hump.

He's just been voted mayor. Last time he was away we started the accordion gags: What's the difference between a squeeze-box and a trampoline? You have to take your boots off to jump on a trampoline.

Codger

I lean silent on the bar, swill my dregs.
I am old fossil to kids who mouth
the language of games and cash: below par,
in bulk, two grand, dead ball kick.
Someone has filled their dreams with balls,
stuffed them full of pound coins.

One, dressed loud in label-talk
is up and down like a toilet seat. One day
he'll be a millionaire, he says, and no one laughs.
I am already half ghost, more overcoat than man.
My hands are marble now. Each time I cough
a fist of sharp lead pencils whacks me in the chest.

We used to say: One day our time will come,
we'll have it all, everything we've dreamed of.
You start off with dreams and finish up with
might-have-beens. But at least we've got
something they can't take away: Inside bogs.
We don't have to shiver when we have a crap.

Once we said: Jerusalem, the National Health.
We said Wemberley and houses free from bugs.
My eyes play back the past and my voice tells me:
What days, what days they were, then, then. No,
I say, enough. I will not dream backwards like a codger.
I screw my eyes tight. I make myself deaf.

Bolero

Not long–not long–not long, says the clock,
eating my hours up tick by tick.

I spin on the carpet's patchy colour
as the world grows dark outside my door.

I see myself there through the haze of years,
way back in the time we claimed as ours.

And again I'm spinning, throwing off weight,
away from the clocks and the dogs of night.

So now I'll do foxtrot, bolero and jig
to shake out the stiffness from shoulder and leg.

Our skin slowly dates to unironed cotton:
those creases we've spent our lives worrying in.

So give me bolero, fandango and reel.
And what if some would mutter *silly* or *fool*?

And if anyone's peeping, well let them gaze.
Sure, I'll give their eyebrows some exercise.

Not long, says the clock, not long d'you hear?
I say: Quiet, you miserable one-song bore!

And give me the tango, bolero and samba,
give me fandango and polka and rumba.

Not long, says the clock, not long before
you get your choice of earth or fire.

And its stiff hands would wave me ta-ta
as I skip away on the beat of time.

In the Public Interest

In the public interest you tuck stale bread
Under your shirt, sneak it down the iron walkways;
When the key-men are still you soak white lumps,
Mould them into the shapes of your silent shrieks.

In the public interest you sup a weekly hooch,
Brewed from potato peel in a hidden bucket,
And blank for one night the musty block,
The tight yard you circle for a single hour each day.

In the public interest you wrap in coarse blankets,
And palm that fierce solitary ache, recall
Through years of wall and curse and clammy dark
The reach and touch of other hands.

In the public interest you press cold flags,
Run the cramped miles between window and door
While others stride the long carpets, white corridors
To harry the grey-suits, the official head-shakers.

In the public interest you welcome odd visitors:
Cockroach and spider, and mould damp bread into
The shapes of your imagined freedom while
You re-make an old tale for a voice not yet found.

The Scene

Ay, this is the scene, this the place:
Early evening, harvest time:
Tractor throbbing slowly through hay
To the churchbells' rippling chime.

A lone bird spills notes, sheep munch grass –
All seems as it has long, long been
As from the swaying lane I look
Across gently rolling shades of green.

A stoat darts into the thistled verge:
Roadside haunt of butterfly,
Rooks wheel over fawn waves of wheat,
An ancient woman clicks pedalling by.

Then from the old mill, newly plush,
The alarm screams out: *Thief! Help! Take care!*
Beware of young men, white or black,
Who have no business lurking here.

Slow Turn

With the slow turn of a dancer he faced away
From the muscle machine and the banter contest,
The room where he'd acted the snarling boy.

Hearing a bird pipe in the hollow of night,
He back-handed the drape, scanned the purple moon-sky,
Saw dark wings slip through the fingers of a tree.

When the lads saw how his eyes would gaze beyond,
They raised the talons of their wit, plunged for the fray.
So his toes kissed the grating boards goodbye.

As the earth clicked its tongue to the rhythm
Of his footsteps, he heard the hills panting nearby,
Sunlight laughing through a wood of bluejays.

The Nature Boys

Work the cliff-face. That's what we do. Our crew.
Each of us a cog a link, a fingery grab.
Bonzo spies the twig-pile through his long glass eye.

Maca does his monkey-boy routine
along the inchy ledges, goes dip-dip-dip,
juggles them down to Oz behind the stumps.

He sends them down the chain of hands
we've thrown across the cliff,
that delivers them to me, still warm.

I heap them up like mounds of cooling pebbles,
build a castle of them in the sand.
And get away with it.

Right underneath the nose of rock
and that big dick of a lighthouse-keeper.
It's a joke. Really. A scream. No kidding.

When the Weather Breaks

For bran-dry weeks the ploughed earth
Has broken into ghost-clouds of grit,
Sheep have nipped at shreds of brown paper,
And clumps of earth have sighed into the river,
While trees whispered of rain,
Of thunder and cloudburst that passed us by.

Now, as the first plump drops
Bacarole on vine and quince,
Dust puts on a patterned smock,
Each fat stone dons a shining head-dress,
And the willow begins to sway,
Does a slow shimmy on the spot.

Rain

The rain has erased the western horizon,
The pasture where tall purple thistles have risen.

The rain is the rivers and seas of the sky.
Now the hill and the highroad are quite washed away.

The copse is an island, the barn roof a boat.
The rain is a big bird, a grey wind-blown sheet.

It has hung glassy beads on twig, stem and branch,
And rinsed out the brightness from mustard and goldfinch.

The rain is a drummer, and Death's ashen curtains,
And the voice of old age that speaks through our bones.

It wraps close around you, a creature of myth
That would draw you far down, deep into the earth.

The rain is a blessing, the rain is a curse:
Sweeping out nestlings from high in the trees.

The rain is a promise, the rain is a song
Releasing a damp zest from nettle and cowdung.

Adrift

As the ship forged on through the empty ocean
All hands on board seemed drugged by calm.
In the peaceful monotony of routine watches
We played our favourite mockery game.

We joked and yarned and talked of great boats,
And mocked the old deckie, the shantyman-poet.
For his wailings and warblings and recitations,
We ribbed him and ragged him to the best of our wit.

'C'mon, give us a song,' we'd say, faces dead straight.
Then when he got singing we'd all start to howl,
Or we'd creep up and catch him tongueing a song
And douse him with dregs from the cat's waterbowl.

'There's history tied up in them songs,' he would say.
'Songs that have helped other people get by,
To live and survive and find strength. And who knows,
You might find that you need them yourselves one day.'

'So who needs old shanties on an oil-fired ship?'
I asked him to a wave of fast-rising chuckles.
'And songs about lovers are strictly for girls,
And poems are for women and men with no balls.'

'Laugh,' he said, 'laugh, laugh your socks down,
Laugh like the fools and idiots you are.'
'Just watch your mouth you silly old bonehead,'
I told him, and gave him a very hard stare.

'I don't want to hear any more of your babble,'
I said waving my finger under his nose.
That shut him up as we powered on through,
Sailing deep into a warm ocean haze.

Then the heat it came on all strong and airless,
And the sea went flat till the wind puffed up.
We gave reefs to the eastward a very wide berth
And secured all loose gear on the rolling ship.

Then the wind turned demon with shrieks and howls,
Came hunting for us from the edge of the world.
High furious seas came crashing on down
Till the ship could no longer be controlled.

We could see not a thing for the hurtling spray,
Our faces were pelted and stung until numb.
Great claws of salt tore through the hatch covers,
Sent shreds flying off like dark birds of doom.

The waves battered on until iron gave way:
Stairways and railings were torn from the starboard,
A funnel was plucked off and tossed over our heads,
What remained of the boat was flung lurching forward.

Sight of the first shark was a blow to the gut.
Then more came lurking, so with fast-drumming hearts
We sent out a desperate SOS,
Freed and lowered the undamaged lifeboats.

Hauling away we watched the ship's death throes,
Saw her bows ride clear and point at the sky.
She rumbled and groaned as her guts exploded,
Then she slipped away through a white boiling sea.

Our small craft managed to ride out the storm.
So, keeping the breeze to the starboard quarter,
To the rhythmical scraping of our two balers,
We watched out for land across calming water.

We saw blurs that swelled to look like islands
Then turn into clouds and go floating away;
Fears were the links of a long iron necklace
That weighed round our necks as we scanned a void sea.

When the fog floated down like an endless grey shroud
Only plashing water broke the hush.
As the stillness grew stiller and ever more quiet
My thoughts jumbled up in a hot swirling hash
Of graveyards and sharks' teeth, corpses and bones.

I saw mighty ghostships of the ocean
Coming straight for us, piling on through,
Till cold sweats and unstoppable trembles came on.

Then the shantyman, he started to sing.
A single voice rose through the gloom.
'Come on now,' he said, 'set your tongues free
And feel your lowdown spirits climb.'

'You laughed,' he said. 'But not any more.
Now you'll sing or fall prey to your very worst fears.'

'Now sing,' he said. 'Sing. Sing for your lives.
Find your lost voices, find your lost songs.
A man has a voice to do more than just mock.
So, come on, lift your heads and fill up your lungs!'

We began as croakers till our throats were cleared
Of dust and rust and years of dross;
Through line and verse our voices grew
Till the froggy crew was loud as a chorus.

We dredged from memory song and tune,
Joined together in ballad and hymn:
Danny Deever, Wild Rover and Blow the Man Down,
For Those In Peril and Jerusalem.

The shantyman sang, conducted, recited:
From the Odyssey and the Ancient Mariner,
The book of St John and The Wreck of the Deutschland;
Shakespeare's Caliban and mad King Lear.

And so kept at bay those private horrors:
Dark visions of havoc and ruination,
Our ghostly skulls in imaginary mirrors;
Until cliffs of fog crumbled into the sea
To reveal a shining watery way
That seemed like the path to our salvation.

Earth Sting

Ices soften, drip and run
trippers ripen in the sun

in harbour trash a chiptray floats
a miniature of upturned boats

the tide come crashing, booms and breaks
rough old music, cue to wakes

sands give way to tidal drag
the lifeguard plants a warning flag

boys dressed up in smiles that mock
go off larking on the rock

claws like broken bottle glass
tear at the cliff's heart as they pass

boulders sigh and pebbles gasp
flesh reels from spray: the water's wasp.

Taken In

Here at the earth's hard crumbled edge
Where certainties of rock are questioned,
Is the power of flux, unfixedness;

Bald heads of quartz, the seaweed-haired,
Are mesmerised and taken in
By a sea the same and ever different
That carries off its own detritus;
Sweeps away starfish, crabs and minnows,

And releases men on amphibian limbs,
Over ropes and under bow, through waterweeds,
Down where dark birds turn into fish;

Down into cool and shifting space,
To stretch and rise for dolphin dives,
To turn and drift in octopus waves,
Relieved of weight a heart sustains,
What makes of skulls such heavy stones.

The Missed Boats

Gull and gullscream down on the baked black weed.
Lash, lash and kickback. Waves with mains of foam roar,
Come dashing to pounce on floating driftwood,
As voracious currents suck the sands away; while far,
Far out, unreachable boats move slowly westward.

Salt hands reach in and scoop up oval stones,
Spin and rattle, let go; come back with a whoosh,
Extending ever further; deep into caves, to turn
More rocks before slipping away murmuring: hush.

The rush and clack, the dance of weed to stony music;
The blue, the green, the blue-green water, sudden
And predictable, washing out to the furthest rock
While a faint boat is drawn along the horizon's line.

Hush. Hush, hush; as more low waves are now unloosed:
Fingers of a skilled masseuse over a skin of grit;
Green satin spread beneath the sun, wafted and released.
The blue-green water rolls, curls and stretches out.

From blue and blue-green water all boats are gone.
Blue-green gives way to blue, and blue to haze,
And haze rubs out with ease that long dividing line,
And sky blends with sea, and sea becomes sky
Where gulls are mere specks that go drifting away.

Waves

I walked away from there still squabbling
with imagined voices, cursing thick skulls;
threatening to go back armed with home truths,
disabuse the nitwit crowd. *And another thing.*

But surf hushes here. Only sandbirds call.
The slow waves ease whispering in, pausing,
turning pebbles round and over, rubbing off
rough edges; stone like sparkling silk.

*Don't tell me about real life. I was sorting problems
while you were still sitting on Old Mother Hubbard's lap!*

The sun paints each wavetop silver. Breeze carries
feathers of song beyond the cliff. Holes in rock
are doorways into years, and fingers of bladderwrack
stretch out, exploring to the edge of the world –

places beyond the last rock, other side of the horizon,
islands reached by sailing boat navigating from the stars.

Those easy waves roll shushing in, spreading long,
transparent, one after another, drawing white curtains,
kissing stone heads, stroking jagged faces,
erasing footprints that go nowhere.

Sardines

Lester Young was the President of sax players.
He knew where to find salvage. His notes were pips
that grew into swaying forests, from which rose
the great birds of myth that drift out
towards the furthest edges of the universe.

Once, I got away, but the road turned into a loop.
She said 'How much did you pay for that thing?
First it was Shakespeare, then scribbly landscapes.
What next? Ballet dancing?' Prez talked gibberish,
but spoke like a saint with that horn at his lips.

He was transformed from a shambles as he began to make
songs from his breath; songs like snakes without venom,
whose skin will whisper to yours of the ache
and the longing and the loss and the worry, and more,
much more: things we cannot find the words to speak.

She said, 'You couldn't even play recorder at school.'
I said, 'Mother, I am not a child, and the money was mine.
And maybe I will never be able to play very well…'
She said, 'You're just like your father. And why
I got stuck with him I do not know. I was such a fool…'

I hear these sounds: tunes that move like dolphins,
that fly and plunge and rise again against the tide;
tunes like the songs of whales, tunes that float, tunes…
She said, 'And don't forget to check the grid's not blocked.
And when you go down the road pick up a tin of sardines.'

Your years are ships that get lost in foggy weather,
and the waves of your dreams leave only flotsam
and feathers. But Prez could spring from the bother
that dumped him on the strandline, surprising you:
expect him to go one way, and he goes another.

Breath

So far out there I cannot see you
With your curved brass horn –
The saxist of the glassy distance.

The wisps of your tune rise and float;
Breath becomes cloud; vapour into feathers –
Pale birds of the glacier country

Where leaves are made of frost
And fields of white powder are crossed
Only by prints of the lone wild cat.

Your spacy notes come wafting through mist,
Drifting over bones and skeleton rafters,
Come flying between pylons,
Breezing in like lone sailors, lost astronauts –
Survival tales of tempest, shark and reef.

The embers of elegy burn in the throat of your horn,
Glowing like distant planets –
New constellations of the stargazers' dreamnight.

Soft pulsing notes fall like paws of the snow leopard.

You who have no body but only song,
I catch your scent line pine from the cold woods.
I feel your breath on my face.

Leaving Town

Time and again you hear chimes from the colonel's watch.
They go tinkle-tinkle, and take you back through his eyes
into the past where something bad has happened.
It's about money and death and who can shoot fastest.
It's like Mexico in Italy with a lot of dust
and mean-looking fellahs in big hats. But Clint,
he's always too sharp for them. He's got mystery
and strength, and nobody messes him around.
He's always between places, no worries about rising damp,
and rot in the windows. And he only says what needs saying.
And if you get a picture of him and look at it real hard,
it's as if he's smiling back like he knows you.
I've always gone for cigars, and not shaved much.
'There's a film about emotional evasiveness
on the other side,' she says. 'Don't you think
it would be a good idea to watch it together?'
Clint and the colonel begin as enemies, and then team up,
and by the time the gang rob the bank in El Paso
yer man is pretending to be one of them.
Nothing stays the same for long. No boring Sundays for him.
'You know the best thing about cowboy films?' she says.
'The cactuses!' Then throws the door wide and huffs out.
So this is it. This is someone's last stand in the dust
with the sun scorching down and trumpets blaring,
and then the chimes starting up in between the brassy stuff.
And upstairs she's thumping about in that special way of hers.
So then you're waiting to see who shoots who.
Then more trumpets and chimes, and then it all goes
dead quiet, and you know that this really is it:
this is where it's all been leading; it's showdown time.
And then the chimes start again. And then Bang!'
The front door slams. The house shudders. And she
is out there
dragging her suitcase
into the street.

One Ear

Let me have the rhythms of the singing voice.
Ay, let me have songs right up till the end.
Don't let me go dressed in leaves of wormwood,
a hat made of aloes and rue.

Don't let me go off, pickling my days in vinegar,
eyes hardened to little pips of rage,
weeping self-sorrowful lemon juice tears.

Let me still have songs when the lights go dim.
And when they've gone out, if anyone is bothered to recall,
let them say I sent few messages in acrid smoke.
And if anyone does claim I was prone to a tipple
of crab apple wine, let them add: But not *too* often.

Then let them say that though I gave up on the mermaid
I went on listening for the nightingale –
which turned out little sweeter than the common blackbird.
But let them say one ear went on listening to the last.

Range

In the house that love rented, they trembled in pillows,
Moved down through the white hills to swim
In salt waters, and lay at the roots of swirling trees,
Until frosts of autumn brought out the leafburners,
And hastened the flight of late passage birds.

The sheets of their bed swooned on the line,
Quivered: a memory of high peaks and virgin snow;
The ghosts of passion withdrawing to leave
Only flags of surrender.

The striped finch sang through its living room bars
Of a time when hair was dancers
On the ballroom of their giddy heads,
Cavorting to a romping tune.

When a bonfire combusted in her belly,
Violins made ropes whose tug she could not resist;
Clothes were skins the bright new snake cast off elsewhere.
A turf of lies almost concealed
The handbag of ashes she carried home.

So they parcelled up their days in routines of pastries,
And orders from the seed catalogue,
As their hearts migrated through the television,
And their hair began turning to string.

Till he slipped through the net of her voice,
Adding his small tread to the noise
That grew from pavement cracks;
Entered the damp and palpable wood
Whose branchtips stretched him skywards
As he eased back into the music of feathers:
A chorus beyond her range;
Her lies, her love, her sentences.

Blue Notes

I knew some women found that image really very sexy.
I was this classic broody guy with guitar and a badge
from the Angst Federation, moaning solos in dark glasses.

But I got wound up so tight, my lines just had to snap.
I was in bits when I first gazed on her. This wild binge:
everyone was getting blasted. Boy, I'd kissed some bottle.

From nowhere this Angel, this glinty-eyed Goddess, appears
talking lyrics and backbeat, saying maybe we two
should boogie some time, maybe we had strong chemistry.

We did blue notes and breaks, some tricky chordwork,
and fingersnaps, and sireny stuff for choruses,
and big vibrato, as we slowly strummed the taut wires.

Then we'd rise to some real expressive pitch, up there
where light comes from, undulating to this lingering,
prolonged, and oh-so-spun-out harmonised crescendo.

When we went to bed I flopped. In a very big way.
She said: 'This has never happened to me before.' I said:
'Nor me. Never. I'm as surprised as you are. Honest.'

She said: 'Well, it doesn't look as if this little fellah
is going out to play tonight.' I laughed. She laughed.
We both laughed. I laughed so much I could have cried.

The Small Laugh

Why has the sex god turned his back and gone?
I will and coax myself to rise, but all in vain.

Those lips say: Tonight, get wild and come.
But only questions surge up through me.

Must a man finish up in a skeleton land
that the caravans of passion have left far behind?

Must I now wear slippers and practise my grumble,
lament the old urge like a boy his lost ball?

Where does it come from, and where does it go?
And why, why, why, does it just up and leave you?

As if you've never once felt the need:
an absence, an ache, a skin the snake's shed.

Is this all that's left of a once handsome tool:
a stump a tossed fag end, a bit of chewed gristle?

I said: Leave it alone woman, let the thing be!
Like trying to stuff toothpaste back in the tube.

Is this how a man ends, when he can't sow his seed:
making a small laugh in which he might hide?

Hymnal

I'd long given up any thought of it. I was
more mindful of slow worms and peach trees.

Oh ay, it came as a big surprise. Although waste
was an evil we were both very much against.

They called us the ghosts, as we tidied the graveyard.
Get close to the dead, though, and you'll learn a lot.

I'm not sure whose idea it was, but we unbuttoned
from Sunday best, lay for warmth, a little touching.

Then she asked, Is this as far as you want to go?
I said: I'm afraid it's more a case of not much choice.

She said, I might just have a recipe for that.
I'll not say what it was, but it had plenty of salt.

It was like one of those speeded-up nature films
where you see a mushroom shoot up from nowhere.

As the old urge came slowly snaking
back through the years and the veins and the bedsheets.

Like tongueing one of Wesley's finest:
no leaving off till you've sung it through.

To the End

When I can no longer tongue
my old out-of-tune songs
will someone touch the lights out.
Don't leave me lying backstage like a dummy.

I've cleared rooms quicker than a rattlesnake
when I've risen to render my party piece.
I've had the big stage beam unplugged
as I creaked up to the highpoint of a turn.

So no one can claim I've not rehearsed for it.

They call me the Serial Warbler,
but my bathroom is La Scala.
Strutting at the kitchen sink,
I'm up there on the biggest boards of all.

So, when I can't manage to mangle a song,
when I can no longer thread the words
along a wobbly rhythm, please,
just knock the light off and say

I went on not-quite singing almost to the end.

Beethoven

I am the unlicked bear, the ugly and half crazy.
I am the tramp who urchins mock and police lock up.
I am the man who breaks pianos as I strain for sound,
as I voyage to the other side to bring back the songs.

I am the misanthrope, the malignant one;
So say those who have small minds and equal knowledge.
But I know if I linger in salons the sharp eyes will see
into my ears where unthinkable weaknesses are hidden.

So my head burns, my skin is aflame, and I who love
the laughter of women must run out into the rain.
Alone, I put on a wild cloak, and walk the wind,
croak out tunes that will swell into symphonies.

Unlike Goethe I bend no knee to title or wealth
for I have ever valued virtue over money. Except,
of course, in dealings with those rogues the publishers,
I say guilt is a curse, a very great evil.

I say: Love demands all, but speech is not adequate.
I say: Let no man be oppressed by another. (But,
who ever had a servant that was not a scoundrel? And, yes,
I did throw a plate of soup at that woodenheaded waiter.)

When I walk alone in the woods, I love humanity most.
Then I say: Let the trumpets sound for all,
let them blow through the cites and the valleys,
let them blast in the darkest corners of the empires.

Fantasies

Beethoven had no children, no natural heir,
but to me he's much more than just a father-figure
because my mother kept his bust in her bedroom.
Some say he died raging, shaking his fist
at a thunderstorm, shouting, 'Comedy is finished!'
And if you knew that colossus the way I do,
then you'd believe it. And you'd agree with him.

I'm working on a piano sonata, struggling
to combine boundless optimism with despair,
then forging through to a visionary conclusion.
We'll have to see. I've got a problem.
But I won't mention my sister-in-law by name:
keeps telling Jean she was off her onion
for breaking with Jack and marrying me.

She says I'm obsessed with a dead man.
Man? Beethoven? Obsessed? Me?
He was a titanic genius, mythical and mesmeric.
Goethe said he was utterly untamed,
and Clementi called him a haughty beauty,
but some believed he was a mad genius,
and others just thought him a hairy tramp.

That woman says I'm a scarecrow and a lunatic,
and when she really gets going she can be quite rude.
No one's exactly sure which year he went deaf,
but sometimes I think he was the lucky one;
plus: it could have freed up his creativity.
You get sudden switches from gloom to light,
ecstatic passion breaking through the calm.

His lovelife, though, was a hopeless tangle.
On the one hand you've got the mysterious letter
to the 'Immortal Beloved', and on the other
the manic possessiveness over his nephew Karl
– fuelled, some say, by a hidden sexual longing –
as he tried to rescue him from the claws of Johanna.
Who was? Guess what? Yes. His sister-in-law.

Sometimes, though, he stopped hating and desired her, too.
But I think we can make sense of the conundrum
because one of his letters to the Archduke Rudolph
speaks of depression and 'moral factors',
and liberation is the central theme of Fidelio.
Anyway, my sister-in-law wouldn't know a crotchet from
a hockey stick, but that doesn't stop her sounding off.

I've heard her say to Jean, 'Why do you stay with him?
You should treat yourself to a bit of fun.'
And we know what old Beethoven would have thought of that.
He tried to create for himself an imaginary family.
He also liked to pretend he was a nobleman.
But some days he stood on the edge of a vast dark pit.
So he knew just where daft, sad fantasies can lead us.

Amen

Green Park is the gang's place now. Spraynames brag and snarl.
The bandstand is a pair of stumps, and the statues have walked;
and Michael thinks that washing-up is done by fairies,
and Sarah smokes and lies about it through her cough,
and Beccy... Yes, Beccy is still that ever ticking tantrum.

And they're all money fiends. As if I have my own machine.
I've been sheltering in the Festival Chorus five years.
Very strict: Don't be late twice, and learn your lines.
I have chains and spyhole. And I go the long way round.
Your breath becomes a Psalm. Rejoice, and you can believe.

You do shouts of anguish in the Chorus, but also joy.
You put on black, and take your place in the long row,
and your voice rises high up there where angels live;
where the skies are never made of ashen clouds,
and the wheeze of autumn doesn't strip the trees to bones.

Gran would take me to the Rose Garden. There was a scent
like mint. You get this lovely flow, all the voices rising.
Bushy Way is another lurking place. But this is a house,
not a jail. You open your throat and sing like a fury.
The rehearsal, though, was rolling when I rushed in.

I'd been playing house detective over missing coins.
And the buses: you wait half a lifetime, then they arrive
in a wagon train. But he pointed me back through the door
saying: Sorry, that's it, you're out, there has to be rules.
I said: No. No, you can't do that. You don't understand.

As if the feather of your voice brushes against
the scented heads of divine flowers
whose perfumed breath, like thyme or lavender,
carries you still higher until you walk across
the night sky using the stars as stepping stones.

And when you arrive
you let go
shouting:
Amen, Amen,
Amen.